# SOLO GUITAR

# a Guitar for Elvis®

Music transcriptions by David Stocker

ISBN 978-1-4234-9663-2

## HAL•LEONARD® CORPORATION

7777 W. BLUEMOUND RD. P.O. BOX 13819 MILWAUKEE, WI 53213

www.elvis.com

Visit Hal Leonard Online at
www.halleonard.com

# All Shook Up

Words and Music by Otis Blackwell and Elvis Presley

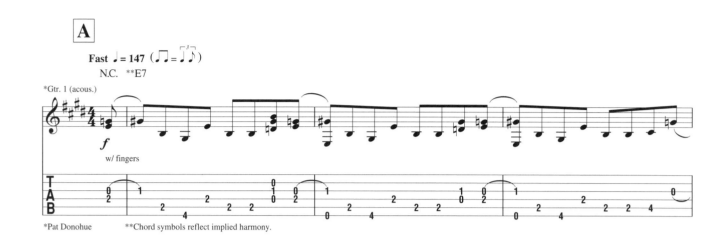

*Gtr. 1 (acous.)

*Pat Donohue        **Chord symbols reflect implied harmony.

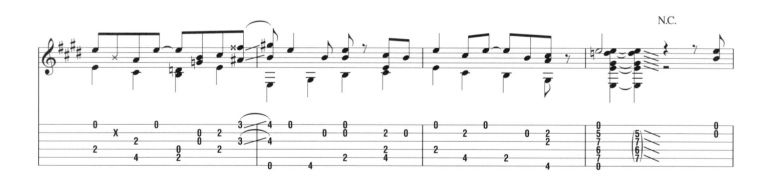

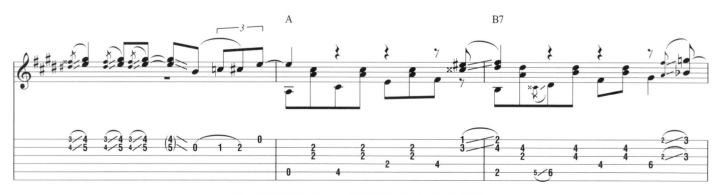

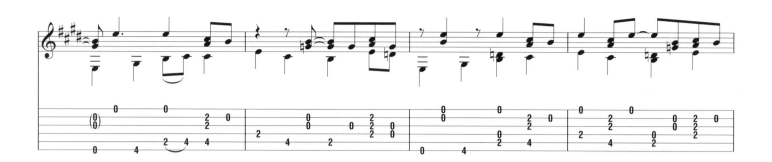

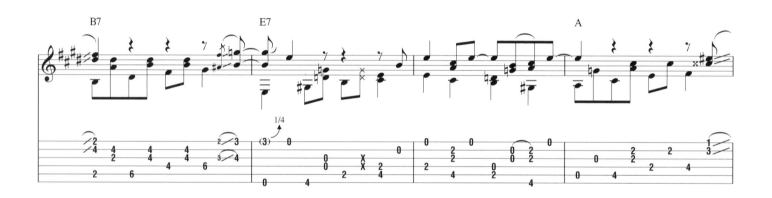

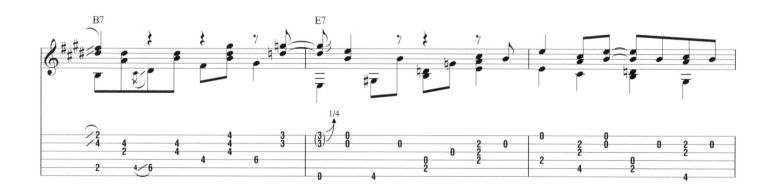

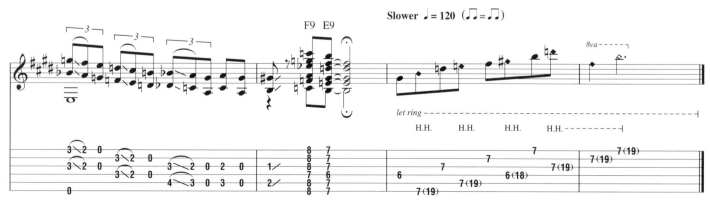

# Mystery Train

Words and Music by Sam C. Phillips and Herman Parker Jr.

*Al Petteway      **Chord symbols reflect implied harmony.

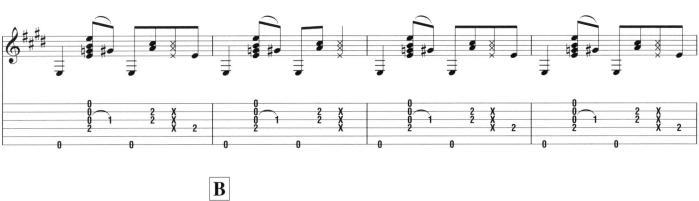

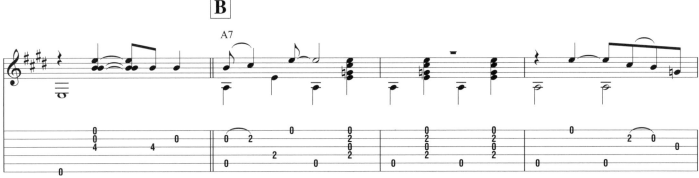

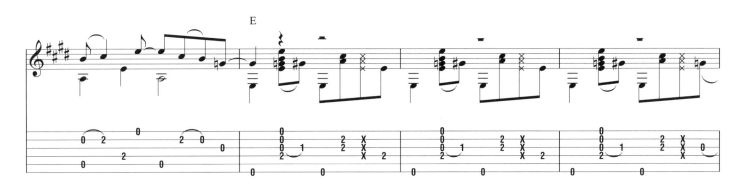

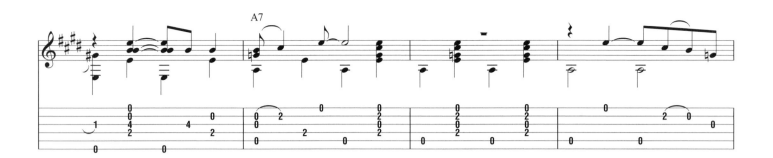

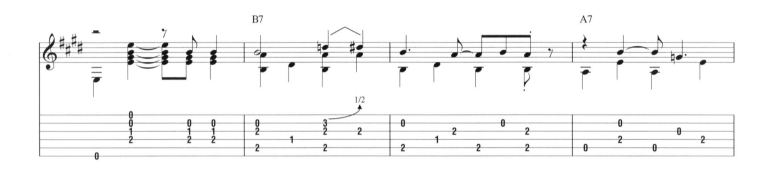

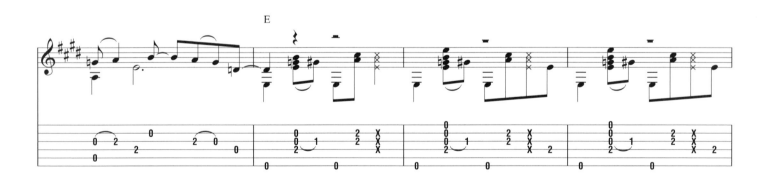

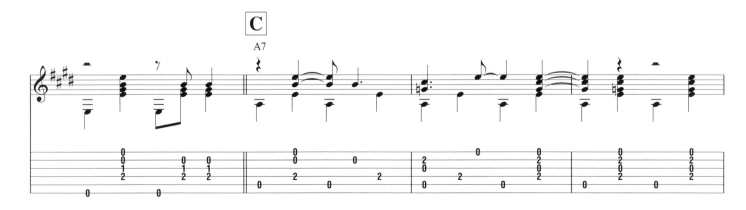

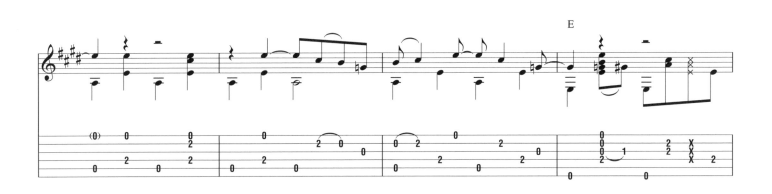

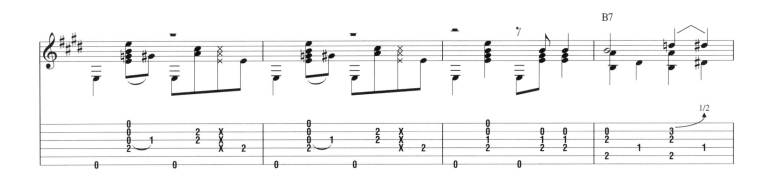

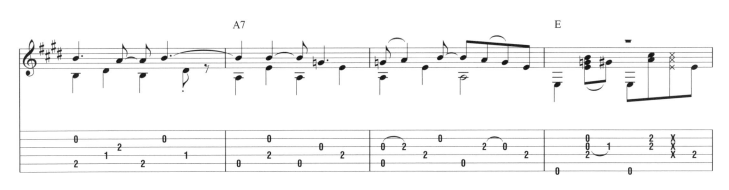

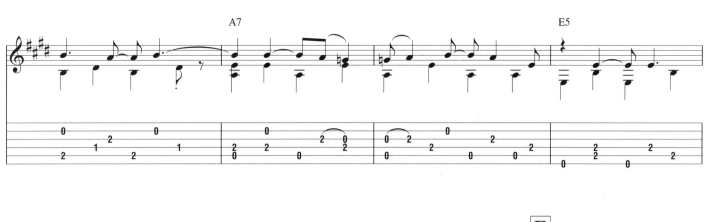

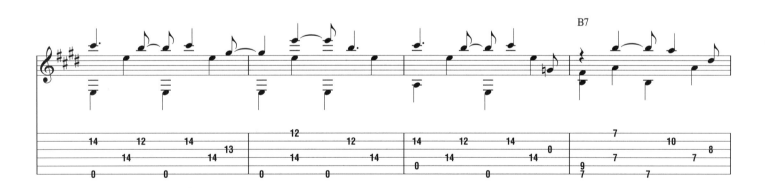

# Can't Help Falling in Love

Words and Music by George David Weiss, Hugo Peretti and Luigi Creatore

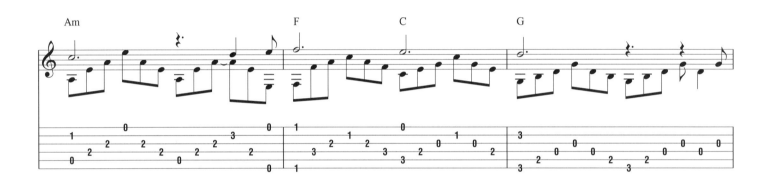

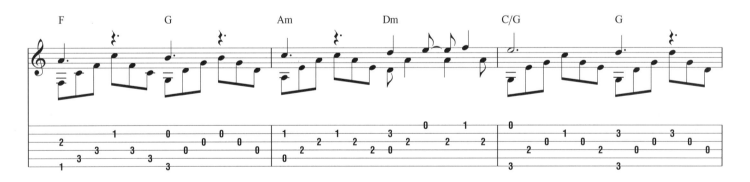

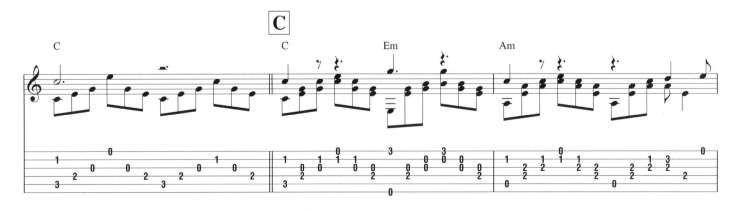

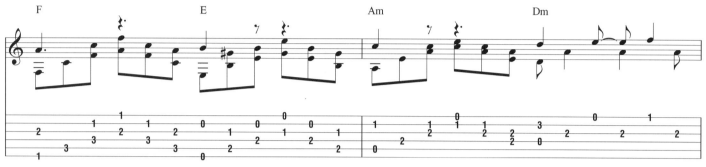

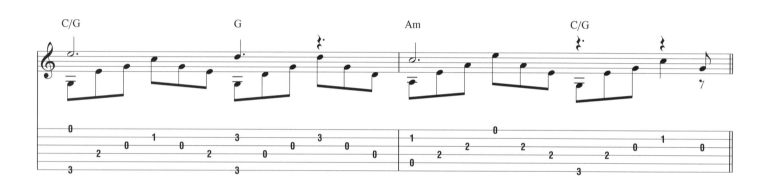

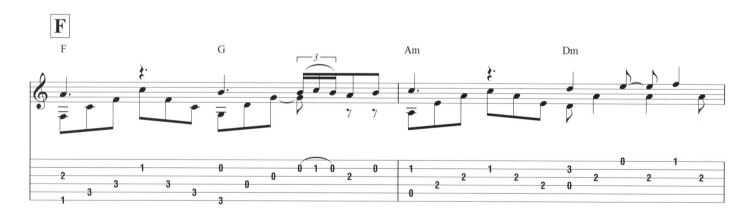

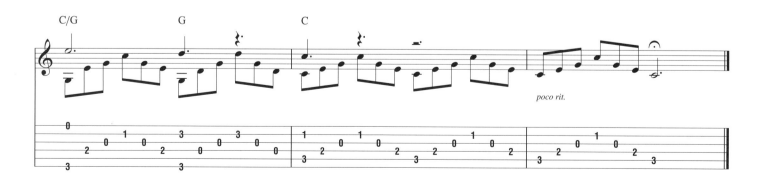

# Suspicious Minds

Words and Music by Francis Zambon

DADGAD tuning:
(low to high) D-A-D-G-A-D

*Laurence Juber

**Chord symbols reflect implied harmony.

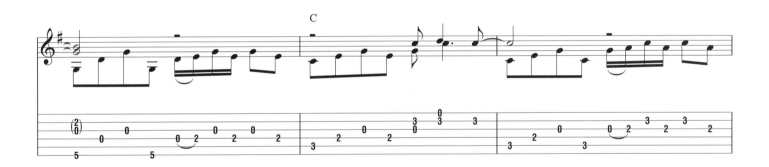

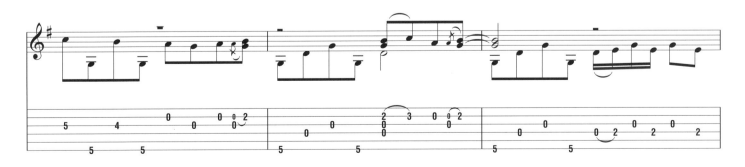

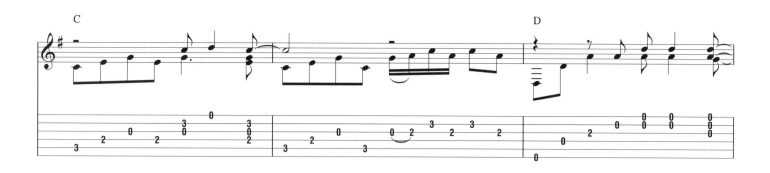

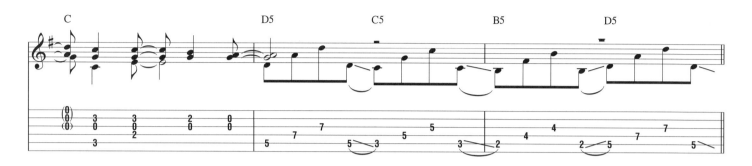

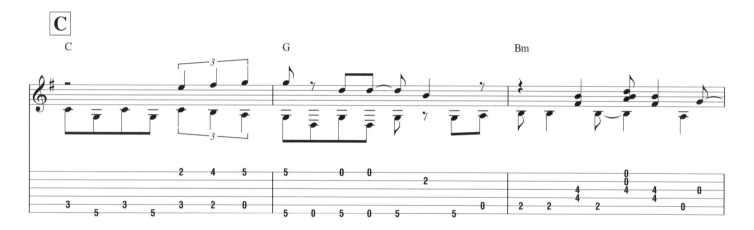

*Slap fretboard w/ right hand

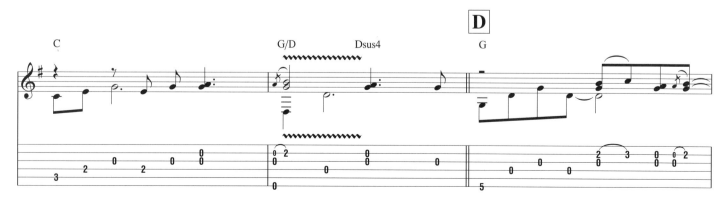

*T = Thumb on 6th string

# Don't

### Words and Music by Jerry Leiber and Mike Stoller

**B**

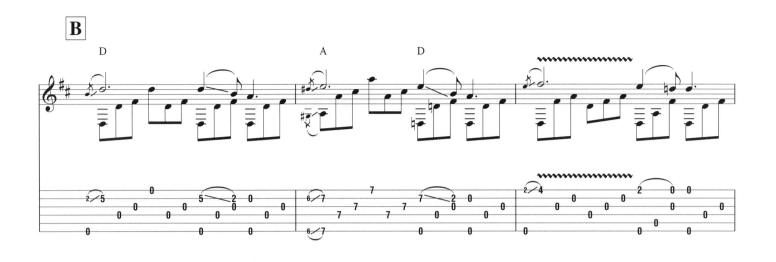

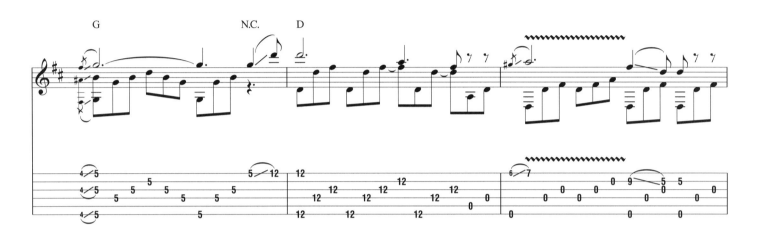

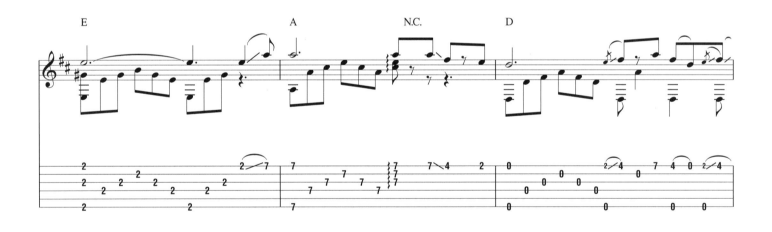

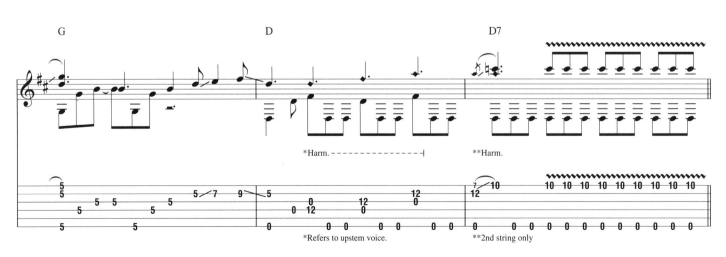

*Refers to upstream voice.

*Harm.

**Harm.

**2nd string only

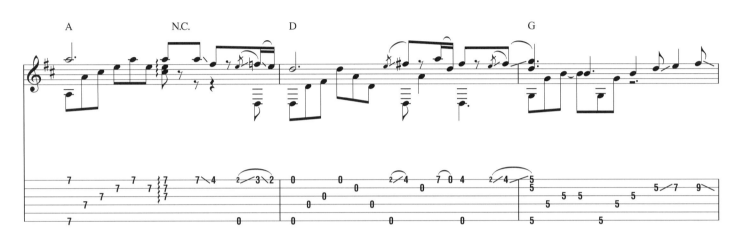

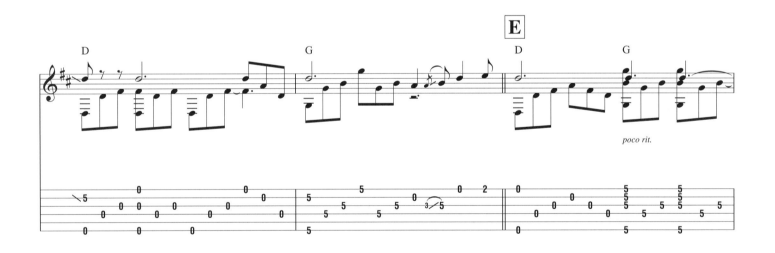

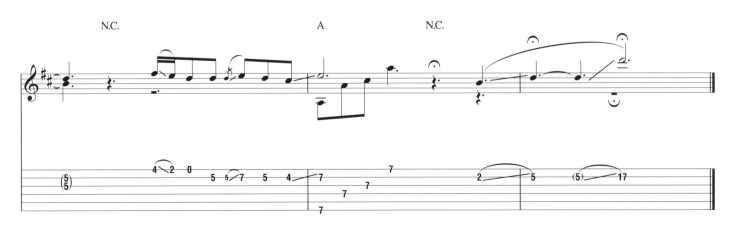

# Heartbreak Hotel

**Words and Music by Mae Boren Axton, Tommy Durden and Elvis Presley**

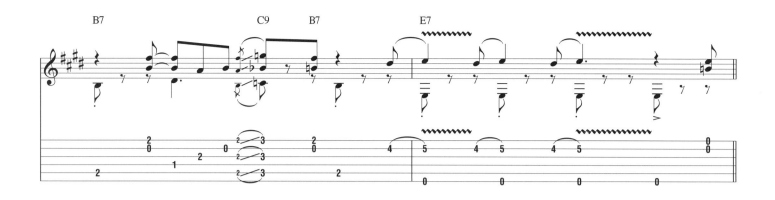

**F**

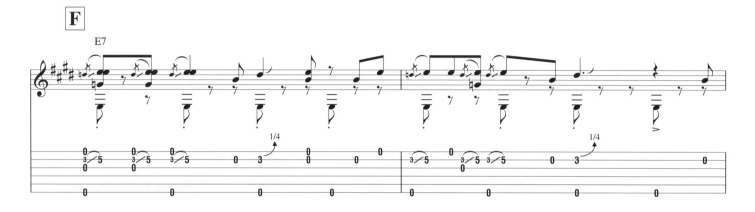

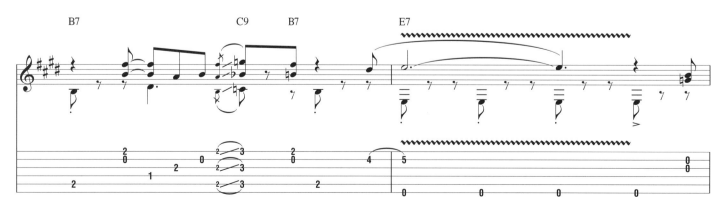

# Little Sister

**Words and Music by Doc Pomus and Mort Shuman**

Open D tuning, down 1 1/2 steps:
(low to high) B↓-F#-B-D#↓-F#-B↓

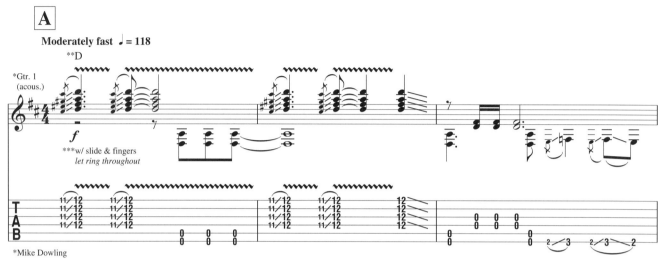

*Mike Dowling

**Chord symbols reflect basic harmony.

***Slide on fret-hand fourth finger. Alternate
between using slide and other fret-hand fingers.

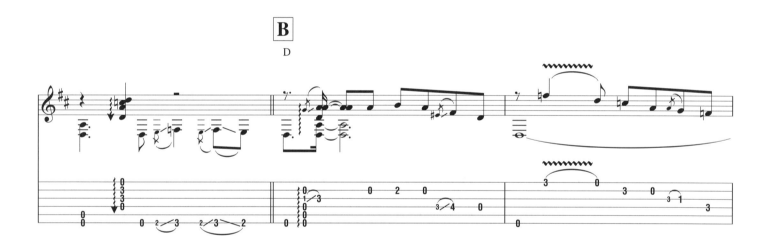

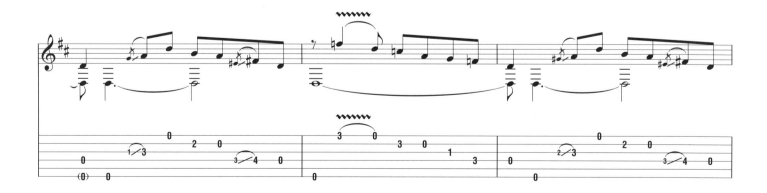

# Don't Be Cruel
# (To a Heart That's True)

**Words and Music by Otis Blackwell and Elvis Presley**

Drop D tuning:
(low to high) D-A-D-G-B-E

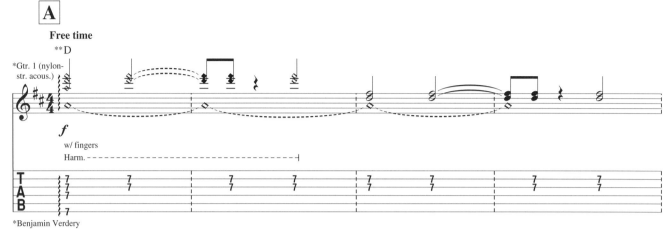

*Benjamin Verdery
**Chord symbols reflect basic harmony.

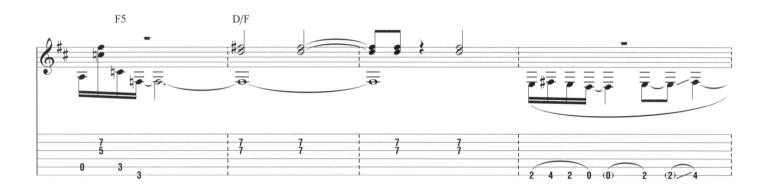

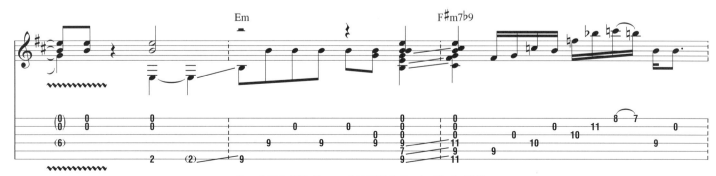

*Upstem voice to left of slash in tab.

*Bartók pizzicato: pluck string forcefully,
allowing it to "snap" back against frets.

# Love Me Tender

**Words and Music by Elvis Presley and Vera Matson**

Open D tuning:
(low to high) D-A-D-F♯-A-D

**A**

Moderately, with rubato ♩ = 77

**Dmaj7

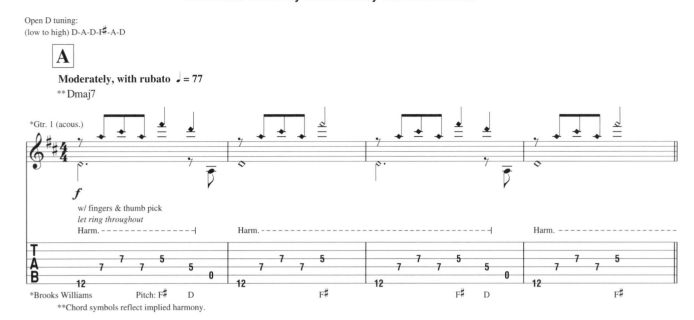

*Gtr. 1 (acous.)

*f*

w/ fingers & thumb pick
*let ring throughout*

*Brooks Williams          Pitch: F♯    D                    F♯              F♯    D              F♯
**Chord symbols reflect implied harmony.

**B**

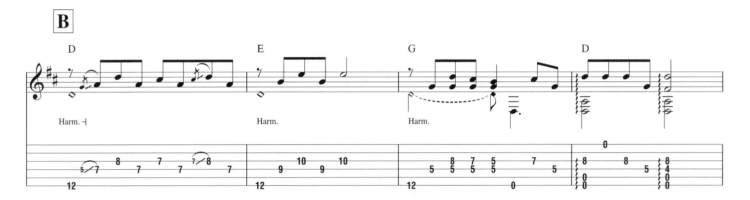

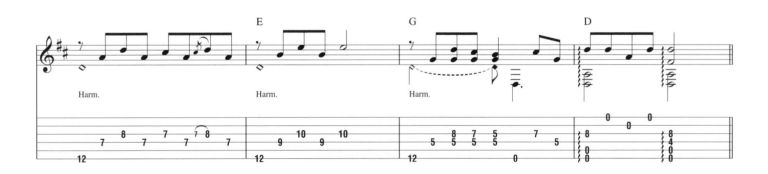

**C**

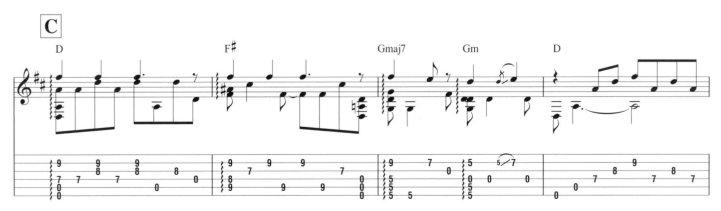

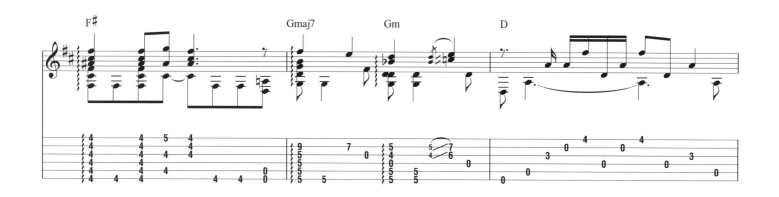

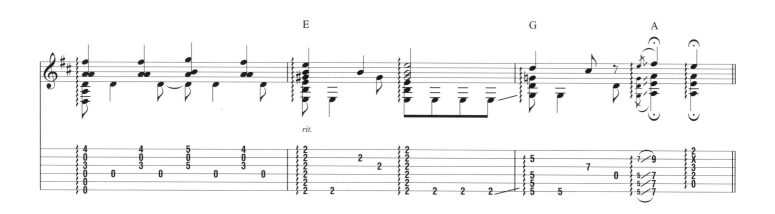

**J**

A tempo

**K**

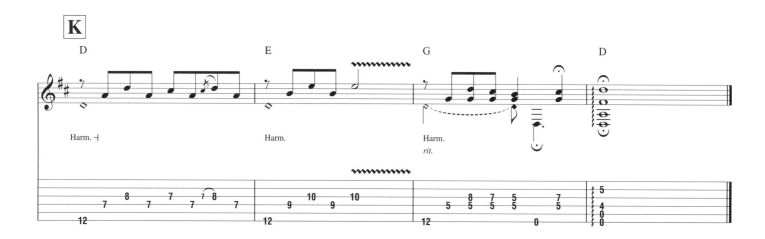

50

# Loving You

### Words and Music by Jerry Leiber and Mike Stoller

*Chord symbols reflect implied harmony.

**Baritone Guitar; sounds two octaves lower than written.

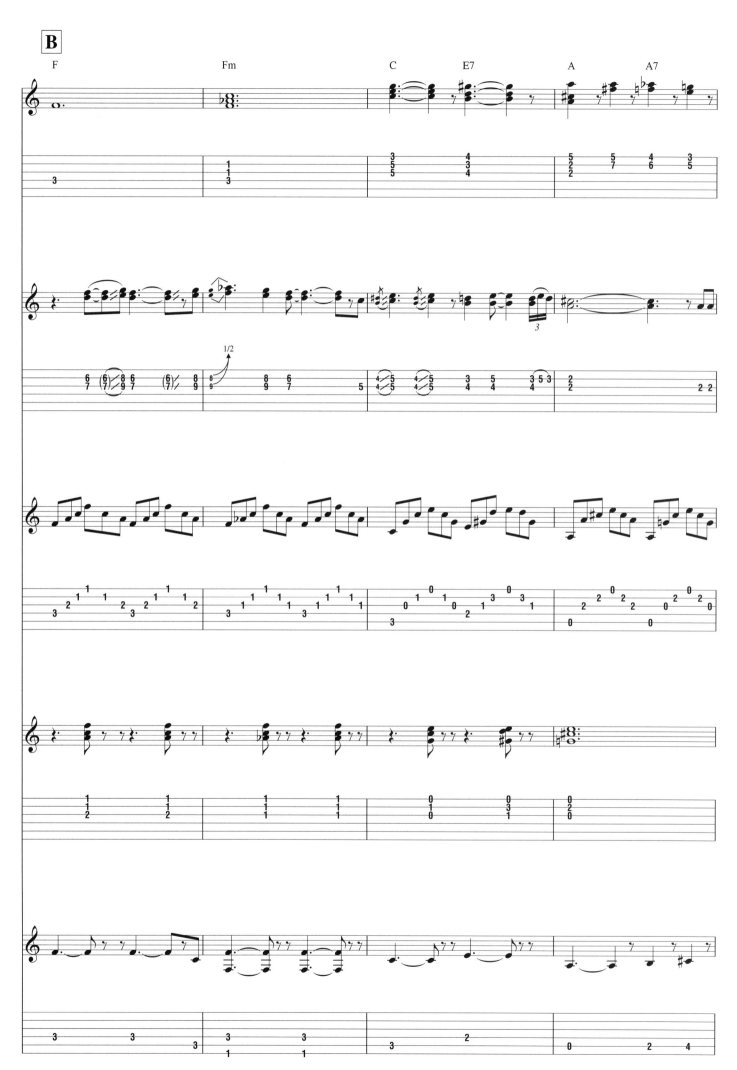

# Hound Dog

Words and Music by Jerry Leiber and Mike Stoller

DADGAD tuning:
(low to high) D-A-D-G-A-D

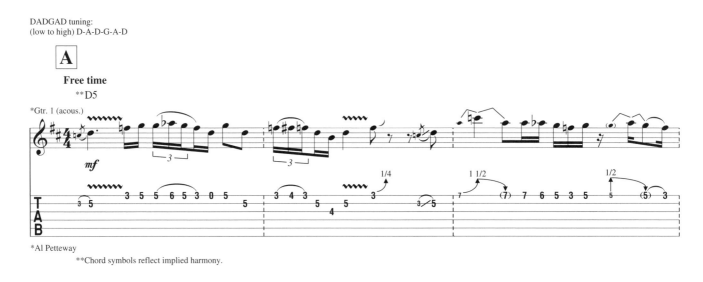

*Al Petteway

**Chord symbols reflect implied harmony.

***Slap pick-hand thumb
against 5th & 6th strings.

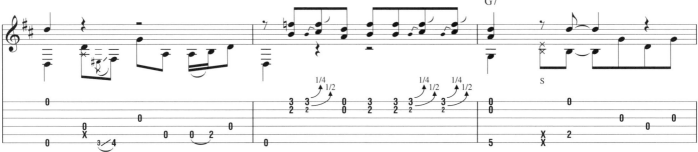

# Jailhouse Rock

**Words and Music by Jerry Leiber and Mike Stoller**

Open G tuning:
(low to high) D-G-D-G-B-D

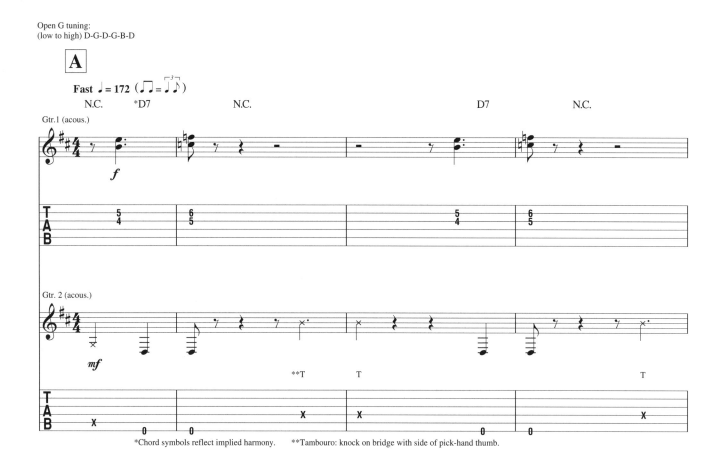

*Chord symbols reflect implied harmony.   **Tambouro: knock on bridge with side of pick-hand thumb.

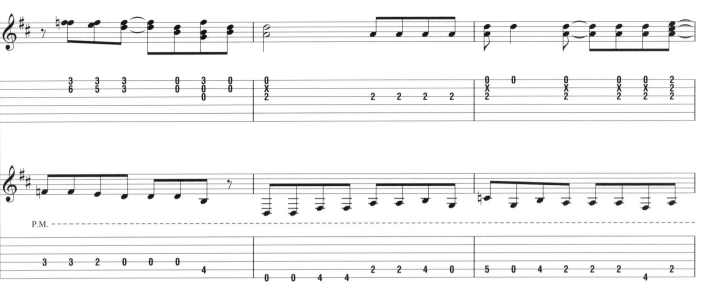

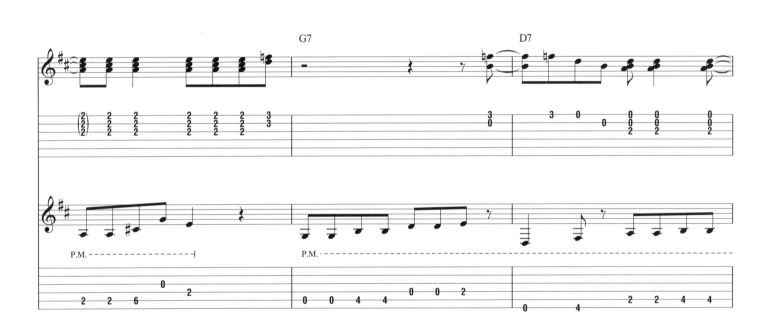

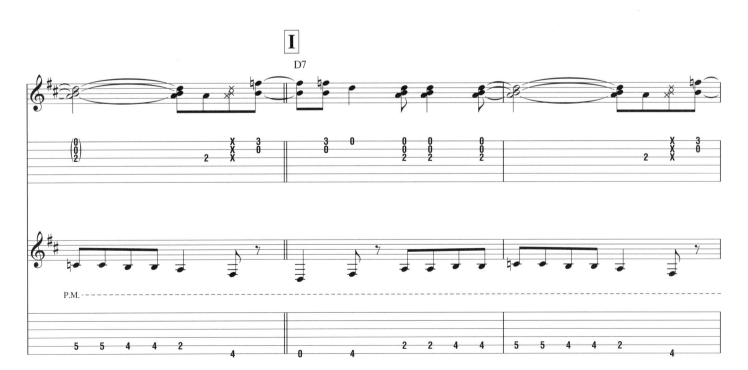

# Are You Lonesome Tonight?

**Words and Music by Roy Turk and Lou Handman**

Open D tuning, down 1 step:
(low to high) C-G-C-E-G-C

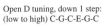

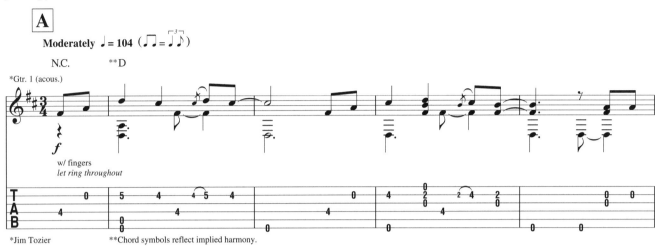

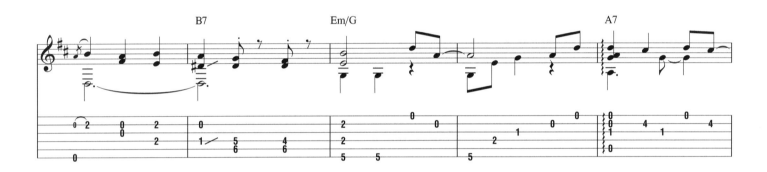

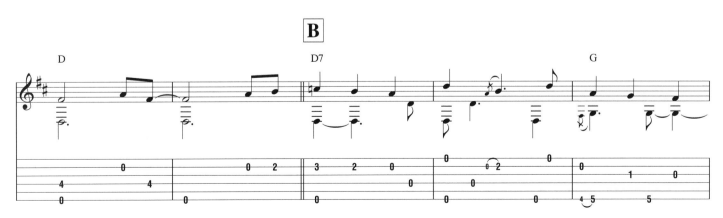

*Played as even eighth-notes.

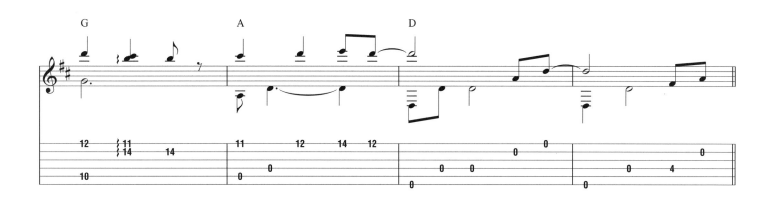

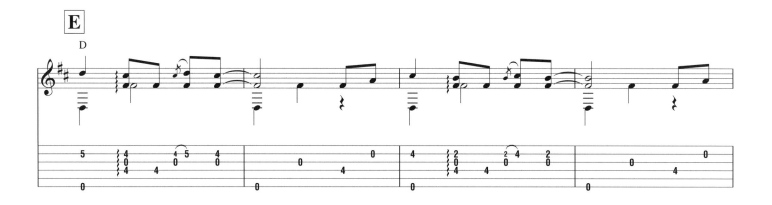

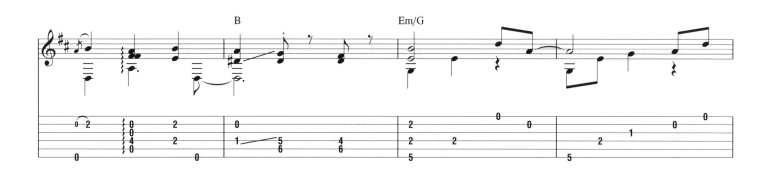

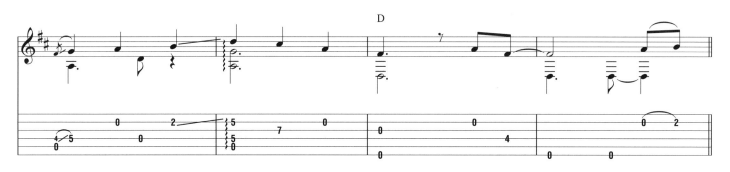

# Viva Las Vegas

### Words and Music by Doc Pomus and Mort Shuman

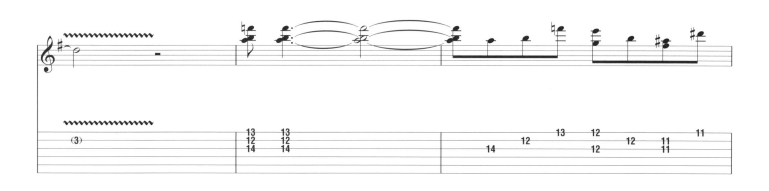

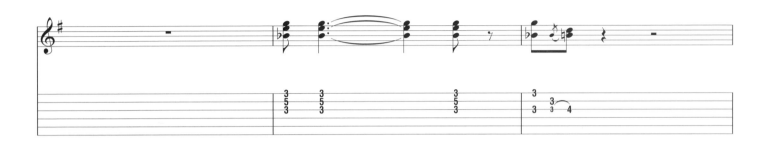

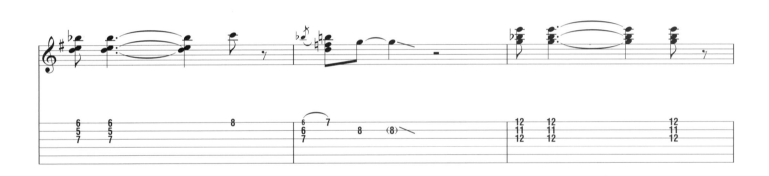

# FINGERPICKING
## GUITAR BOOKS

*Hone your fingerpicking skills with these great songbooks featuring solo guitar arrangements in standard notation and tablature. The arrangements in these books are carefully written for intermediate-level guitarists. Each song combines melody and harmony in one superb guitar fingerpicking arrangement. Each book also includes an introduction to basic fingerstyle guitar.*

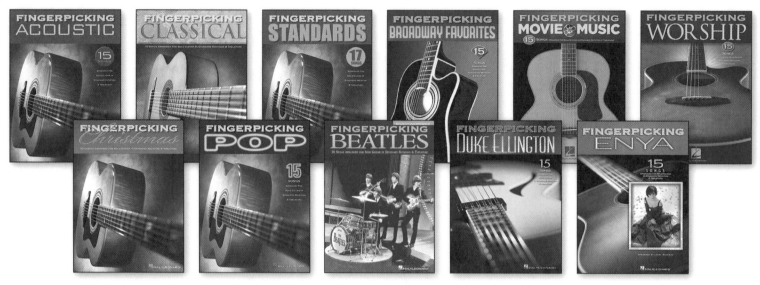

**FINGERPICKING ACOUSTIC**
00699614.................................................................$10.99

**FINGERPICKING ACOUSTIC ROCK**
00699764...................................................................$9.99

**FINGERPICKING BACH**
00699793...................................................................$8.95

**FINGERPICKING BALLADS**
00699717...................................................................$9.99

**FINGERPICKING BEATLES**
00699049.................................................................$19.99

**FINGERPICKING BROADWAY FAVORITES**
00699843...................................................................$9.99

**FINGERPICKING BROADWAY HITS**
00699838...................................................................$7.99

**FINGERPICKING CELTIC FOLK**
00701148...................................................................$7.99

**FINGERPICKING CHILDREN'S SONGS**
00699712...................................................................$9.99

**FINGERPICKING CHRISTMAS**
00699599...................................................................$8.95

**FINGERPICKING CHRISTMAS CLASSICS**
00701695...................................................................$7.99

**FINGERPICKING CLASSICAL**
00699620...................................................................$8.95

**FINGERPICKING COUNTRY**
00699687...................................................................$9.99

**FINGERPICKING DISNEY**
00699711...................................................................$9.95

**FINGERPICKING DUKE ELLINGTON**
00699845...................................................................$9.99

**FINGERPICKING ENYA**
00701161...................................................................$9.99

**FINGERPICKING HYMNS**
00699688...................................................................$8.95

**FINGERPICKING ANDREW LLOYD WEBBER**
00699839...................................................................$9.99

**FINGERPICKING MOVIE MUSIC**
00699919...................................................................$9.99

**FINGERPICKING MOZART**
00699794...................................................................$8.95

**FINGERPICKING POP**
00699615...................................................................$9.99

**FINGERPICKING PRAISE**
00699714...................................................................$8.95

**FINGERPICKING ROCK**
00699716...................................................................$9.99

**FINGERPICKING STANDARDS**
00699613...................................................................$9.99

**FINGERPICKING WEDDING**
00699637...................................................................$9.99

**FINGERPICKING WORSHIP**
00700554...................................................................$7.99

**FINGERPICKING YULETIDE**
00699654...................................................................$9.99

FOR MORE INFORMATION, SEE YOUR LOCAL MUSIC DEALER,
OR WRITE TO:

**HAL•LEONARD®**
**CORPORATION**
7777 W. BLUEMOUND RD. P.O. BOX 13819 MILWAUKEE, WI 53213

Visit Hal Leonard online at **www.halleonard.com**

Prices, contents and availability subject to change without notice.

0910

# HAL•LEONARD GUITAR PLAY•ALONG

This series will help you play your favorite songs quickly and easily. Just follow the tab and listen to the CD to hear how the guitar should sound, and then play along using the separate backing tracks. Mac or PC users can also slow down the tempo without changing pitch by using the CD in their computer. The melody and lyrics are included in the book so that you can sing or simply follow along.

INCLUDES TAB

VOL. 1 – ROCK                      00699570 / $16.99
VOL. 2 – ACOUSTIC                  00699569 / $16.95
VOL. 3 – HARD ROCK                 00699573 / $16.95
VOL. 4 – POP/ROCK                  00699571 / $16.99
VOL. 5 – MODERN ROCK               00699574 / $16.99
VOL. 6 – '90s ROCK                 00699572 / $16.99
VOL. 7 – BLUES                     00699575 / $16.95
VOL. 8 – ROCK                      00699585 / $12.95
VOL. 9 – PUNK ROCK                 00699576 / $14.95
VOL. 10 – ACOUSTIC                 00699586 / $16.95
VOL. 11 – EARLY ROCK               00699579 / $14.95
VOL. 12 – POP/ROCK                 00699587 / $14.95
VOL. 13 – FOLK ROCK                00699581 / $14.95
VOL. 14 – BLUES ROCK               00699582 / $16.95
VOL. 15 – R&B                      00699583 / $14.95
VOL. 16 – JAZZ                     00699584 / $15.95
VOL. 17 – COUNTRY                  00699588 / $15.95
VOL. 18 – ACOUSTIC ROCK            00699577 / $15.95
VOL. 19 – SOUL                     00699578 / $14.95
VOL. 20 – ROCKABILLY               00699580 / $14.95
VOL. 21 – YULETIDE                 00699602 / $14.95
VOL. 22 – CHRISTMAS                00699600 / $15.95
VOL. 23 – SURF                     00699635 / $14.95
VOL. 24 – ERIC CLAPTON             00699649 / $16.95
VOL. 25 – LENNON & McCARTNEY       00699642 / $14.95
VOL. 26 – ELVIS PRESLEY            00699643 / $14.95
VOL. 27 – DAVID LEE ROTH           00699645 / $16.95
VOL. 28 – GREG KOCH                00699646 / $14.95
VOL. 29 – BOB SEGER                00699647 / $14.95
VOL. 30 – KISS                     00699644 / $16.99
VOL. 31 – CHRISTMAS HITS           00699652 / $14.95
VOL. 32 – THE OFFSPRING            00699653 / $14.95
VOL. 33 – ACOUSTIC CLASSICS        00699656 / $16.95
VOL. 34 – CLASSIC ROCK             00699658 / $16.95
VOL. 35 – HAIR METAL               00699660 / $16.95
VOL. 36 – SOUTHERN ROCK            00699661 / $16.95
VOL. 37 – ACOUSTIC METAL           00699662 / $16.95
VOL. 38 – BLUES                    00699663 / $16.95
VOL. 39 – '80s METAL               00699664 / $16.99
VOL. 40 – INCUBUS                  00699668 / $17.95
VOL. 41 – ERIC CLAPTON             00699669 / $16.95
VOL. 42 – CHART HITS               00699670 / $16.95
VOL. 43 – LYNYRD SKYNYRD           00699681 / $17.95

VOL. 44 – JAZZ                     00699689 / $14.95
VOL. 45 – TV THEMES                00699718 / $14.95
VOL. 46 – MAINSTREAM ROCK          00699722 / $16.95
VOL. 47 – HENDRIX SMASH HITS       00699723 / $19.95
VOL. 48 – AEROSMITH CLASSICS       00699724 / $16.99
VOL. 49 – STEVIE RAY VAUGHAN       00699725 / $16.95
VOL. 50 – NÜ METAL                 00699726 / $14.95
VOL. 51 – ALTERNATIVE '90s         00699727 / $12.95
VOL. 52 – FUNK                     00699728 / $14.95
VOL. 53 – DISCO                    00699729 / $14.99
VOL. 54 – HEAVY METAL              00699730 / $14.95
VOL. 55 – POP METAL                00699731 / $14.95
VOL. 56 – FOO FIGHTERS             00699749 / $14.95
VOL. 57 – SYSTEM OF A DOWN         00699751 / $14.95
VOL. 58 – BLINK-182                00699772 / $14.95
VOL. 59 – GODSMACK                 00699773 / $14.95
VOL. 60 – 3 DOORS DOWN             00699774 / $14.95
VOL. 61 – SLIPKNOT                 00699775 / $14.95
VOL. 62 – CHRISTMAS CAROLS         00699798 / $12.95
VOL. 63 – CREEDENCE CLEARWATER REVIVAL   00699802 / $16.99
VOL. 64 – THE ULTIMATE OZZY OSBOURNE     00699803 / $16.99
VOL. 65 – THE DOORS                00699806 / $16.99
VOL. 66 – THE ROLLING STONES       00699807 / $16.95
VOL. 67 – BLACK SABBATH            00699808 / $16.99
VOL. 68 – PINK FLOYD – DARK SIDE OF THE MOON   00699809 / $16.99
VOL. 69 – ACOUSTIC FAVORITES       00699810 / $14.95
VOL. 70 – OZZY OSBOURNE            00699805 / $16.99
VOL. 71 – CHRISTIAN ROCK           00699824 / $14.95
VOL. 72 – ACOUSTIC '90S            00699827 / $14.95
VOL. 73 – BLUESY ROCK              00699829 / $16.99
VOL. 74 – PAUL BALOCHE             00699831 / $14.95
VOL. 75 – TOM PETTY                00699882 / $16.99
VOL. 76 – COUNTRY HITS             00699884 / $14.95
VOL. 78 – NIRVANA                  00700132 / $14.95
VOL. 80 – ACOUSTIC ANTHOLOGY       00700175 / $19.95
VOL. 81 – ROCK ANTHOLOGY           00700176 / $22.99

VOL. 82 – EASY SONGS               00700177 / $12.99
VOL. 83 – THREE CHORD SONGS        00700178 / $14.99
VOL. 84 – STEELY DAN               00700200 / $16.99
VOL. 85 – THE POLICE               00700269 / $16.99
VOL. 86 – BOSTON                   00700465 / $16.99
VOL. 87 – ACOUSTIC WOMEN           00700763 / $14.99
VOL. 88 – GRUNGE                   00700467 / $16.99
VOL. 91 – BLUES INSTRUMENTALS      00700505 / $14.99
VOL. 92 – EARLY ROCK INSTRUMENTALS 00700506 / $12.99
VOL. 93 – ROCK INSTRUMENTALS       00700507 / $14.99
VOL. 96 – THIRD DAY                00700560 / $14.95
VOL. 97 – ROCK BAND                00700703 / $14.99
VOL. 98 – ROCK BAND                00700704 / $14.95
VOL. 99 – ZZ TOP                   00700762 / $14.99
VOL. 100 – B.B. KING               00700466 / $14.99
VOL. 102 – CLASSIC PUNK            00700769 / $14.99
VOL. 103 – SWITCHFOOT              00700773 / $16.99
VOL. 104 – DUANE ALLMAN            00700846 / $16.99
VOL. 106 – WEEZER                  00700958 / $14.99
VOL. 108 – THE WHO                 00701053 / $14.99
VOL. 109 – STEVE MILLER            00701054 / $14.99
VOL. 111 – JOHN MELLENCAMP         00701056 / $14.99
VOL. 113 – JIM CROCE               00701058 / $14.99
VOL. 114 – BON JOVI                00701060 / $14.99
VOL. 115 – JOHNNY CASH             00701070 / $14.99
VOL. 116 – THE VENTURES            00701124 / $14.99
VOL. 119 – AC/DC CLASSICS          00701356 / $14.99
VOL. 120 – PROGRESSIVE ROCK        00701457 / $14.99
VOL. 123 – LENNON & McCARTNEY ACOUSTIC   00701614 / $16.99

**Complete song lists available online.**

*Prices, contents, and availability subject to change without notice.*

FOR MORE INFORMATION, SEE YOUR LOCAL MUSIC DEALER, OR WRITE TO:

HAL•LEONARD® CORPORATION
7777 W. BLUEMOUND RD. P.O. BOX 13819 MILWAUKEE, WI 53213

Visit Hal Leonard online at www.halleonard.com

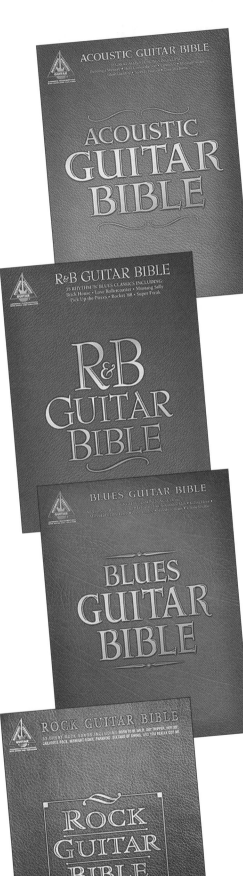

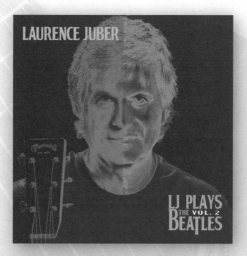
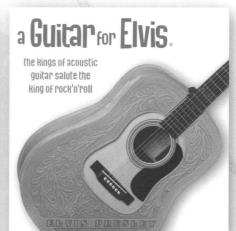
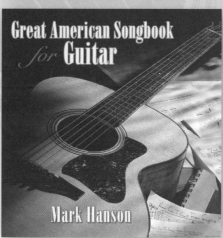
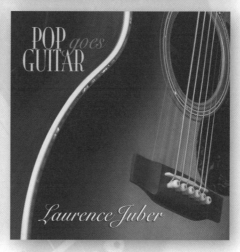